MEN,
WOMEN AND
DOGS

BOOKS BY JAMES THURBER

James Thurber

MEN, WOMEN AND DOGS

WITH A NEW INTRODUCTION BY WILFRID SHEED

DODD, MEAD & COMPANY
NEW YORK

Library of Congress Cataloging in Publication Data

Thurber, James, 1894–1961.
    Men, women and dogs.

    I. Title.
NC1429.T48   1975   741.5'973   75–24914
ISBN 0-396-07206-2

TO ANDY WHITE

who picked up the first of these restless scrawls from the floor fifteen years ago and bravely set about the considerable task of getting them published, this book is gratefully and affectionately dedicated.

ACKNOWLEDGMENT

All the captioned drawings published in this book were first printed in *The New Yorker*. Most of the spots also appeared in the same magazine with the exception of a few drawn especially for this book by James Thurber.

CONTENTS

INTRODUCTION

Thurber in his heyday was one of those international names, like Garbo, Blip or Mussolini, that immediately summoned up a point of view: partly, no doubt, because he sounded like one of his own characters (as did Benchley, Perelman and Damon Runyon—comic writers seem to begin with their own names and build on that) but more certainly because of his drawings. These were mostly drawn in the 1930's—a Golden Age for American humor, mainly because everything else was going so badly. The wisecrack was the basic American sentence because there were so many things that could not be said any other way.

Dorothy Parker's original introduction to this volume is itself a period piece, as enviable and unreachable as a face in a train window. In real life, Thurber was then reeling from one eye operation to another, losing en route most of his sight and his mental perspective, while for Parker's problems, personal and political, you would have needed a broadminded abacus. Yet you won't hear a whimper of this in her essay. For the occasion, she has put on the old greasepaint of the 1920's belletrist to toast the new magic man in town, Mr. James Thurber, a man without a past, a background, or even a physical existence.

These conventions of concealment and artifice were as good for humor as they were bad for sex (n.b., the orgy of film comedies brought on by censorship in the 1930's). As in Victorian England, the clowns were still freer than most people; Lewis Carroll and Edward Lear could bring the Psyche news it would only tolerate from a Jester, and Thurber did the same for us in the puritan twilight of the Depression. The one restriction on such humorists is that they have to tell it in code—the more frabjous the better. Carroll's "slithy toves that gire and gimble in the wabe" are like a message from a prison camp. So *that's* what's going on in there.

Thurber's words alone seldom hit quite that kind of black magic, but combined with his pictures they do it repeatedly. Like Disney and later Walt Kelly and Charles Schultz, he produced universal archetypes fit for a T-shirt. But fine as Pogo and Snoopy are, they do not wake you with palms sweating the way Thurber's people do. Beginning as a *New Yorker* staff man from Ohio, who learned sophistication from E. B. White, like boys smoking corn silk in back of the barn, and staying pretty much within the stylized limits of that magazine, he stumbled upon a vision of man, woman and dog that even an Eskimo (perhaps especially an Eskimo) would recognize and run from.

Thurber was a marvelous comic writer, but alone among such he was able to sketch the phantasmogoric goo from which his funny ideas came. If Henry James or Dostoevsky had done their own illustrations, the results could hardly have been stranger or more illuminating. *Men, Women and Dogs* is like a writer's head with the back open; the fact that it's *funny* back there is as spooky as anything in Jung. Thurber did not make up his jokes in his mouth, like so many clowns, but somewhere between the optic nerve and the unconscious, an area where the slightest tilt can lead to torment and madness.

As it did, we now know, in his last years. But this book belongs to the sunny period before he literally lost his sight and had to move into his own skull for good, with no fresh images to lighten the nightmares. At this point his defective eyesight was still an asset conjuring up useful if scary visions of Rear Admirals on bicycles and dogs guarding window ledges, which he describes in one of his essays.

Characteristically, Thurber made light of his drawings. A man likes to be responsible for his own creations and these were, in a literal sense, "found art." The remarkable E. B. White, having taught him how to write prose, and having turned him in the process from a bumpkin into a byword in sophistication, proceeded in the late 1920's to scoop up his doodles and turn him into an artist as well, whose non-mastery of line came out magically close to Matisse in at least some critics' opinions.

Someday White's role as a hayseed Professor Higgins will be fully acknowledged for the artistic miracle it was (Thurber's early letters show not one trace of his masterful urbanity and his last blustering years demonstrate how paper thin it had been all along) but the subject right now is Thurber and the particular gifts he brought to the operation: fitting White's neat prose to his own wild dreams of men and women until his master was comfortably distanced. The captions of his cartoons are not always so far from the stuff that White used to write for the *New Yorker* under news breaks (e.g., from memory—

News-break "And then little Diggins, only 15 pounds, scored the winning touch-down." White: "little old Diggins, by Gad!") but the total effect was quite different when acted out by Thurber's unbaked cookies (as Parker called them) in befuddled alignment.

Although Thurber's prose had its own unique glories, it could not endure the loss of his sight as White's surely could have, but fell off tragically and bewilderedly. There was a brief, gallant period in the early 1940's when he mustered his last clear visual memories and produced at frantic speed his finest work. Then a period of wild word-play in which he strove vainly to make the words do it all but couldn't quite swing it. And finally those last stories in which people pour drinks upon drinks, and the author can no longer *see* things for them to do.

So his comic genius hung by a thread to his flickering vision, which had already been cruelly reduced by a childhood accident involving a bow and arrow. His life was in fact a sickeningly literal enactment of The Wound and the Bow theory (namely, that to draw the magic bow of art, one must have a disabling wound). Thurber's wound gave him a funny looking world to draw and write about, and then his wound took it away again.

Thus the beguilingly blurred figures undercut by the incisive voice of the half-blind man, perhaps not quite sure where he is even in his own drawings. Some of these pictures are downright accidental. The notorious first Mrs. Harris (p. 143) was supposed to be crouched on a staircase not a bookcase: but it seems the artist's perspective failed him into a masterpiece. No wonder Thurber downplayed his art. Yet an openness to the accidental is a mark of genius. And precisely because it is accidental, Thurber blunders into effects beyond the reach of controlled draftsmanship. (For the last months of Walt Kelly's noble life, someone else did his drawing for him. But who could imitate Thurber's mistakes?)

Yet if his eyes were a crucial part of his comic machine, they were not the only part; his ears were in there too. The blurry women who menace the Thurber male, and the shaggy dogs that comfort him, are respectively strident and quiet as snow. In real life, Thurber was surrounded by his share of menacing women, starting with his mother, who set the trend, and one imagines their voices crackling out of the fog as harshly as the blind man's crackles back at them. But it is too simple to say that Thurber hated women. A close look at the creatures he drew suggests a fondness and a bizarre companionship. If some of his women are a bit on the tough side, they need to be to help the

Thurber male across the street. (This would be a screaming grievance later when, in real life, he had to be led to the bathroom, but shouldn't be read back too far. In this book men and women carry each other inexplicably home about equally often, and the monsters are more than made up for by gentle spirits "from haunts of coot and hearn" and good-hearted blondes and nude pianists.) Although the Thurber woman is most triumphantly herself as the back part of a house lunging toward an apprehensive male, she is not always herself.

At his crudest ("Goddamn pussycats"), Thurber reflects the hearty misogyny of the frontier, echoing Mark Twain and his own boss, Harold Ross, who periodically blamed the state of the nation on women schoolteachers. As such he is merely a footnote to social history: sensitive boys from the *Macho* country, blaming their mothers for making them sissies and lunging around speakeasies getting even with Wellesley girls and other effete Easterners.

But his feeling for women is usually more complicated than that. Their abiding gift is the power to baffle; Thurber's women may be illogical, but they are seldom stupid—and there is always a sense that they are probably right, that they "know" something. This imputation of mystical qualities may still be maddening to feminists, but at least Thurber's women are never inferior, and his response to them is closer to fear than contempt.

Furthermore, in emphasizing his alleged hatred of women, commentators have overlooked his equal and similar hatred of men. Riffling through the cartoons again, one notes that the males are just as liable to wild flights of illogic and of fiendish malice as the females. The only constant is warfare, culminating in the crashing cadenza in the back, "The War between men and women." Yet even this is complicated by strange collusions and crossings of sex lines. The dreadful Thurber couple hunting in pairs puts in several appearances: e.g., the unholy twosome who have broken into someone's apartment to perform their mad dance ("I don't know them either, dear, but there may be some very simple explanation.")

Checking with Thurber's prose pieces, one finds the same people with the gloves (Thurber's) off: the couples who stay all night, zestfully wrecking homes and marriages, the swinish practical jokers and dotty women poker players, and—significantly often—a goodly measure of men picking on men. Life for Thurber was as competitive as it was for any hustling midwesterner or for those compulsive games players in the Algonquin set, but it was softened by his goofy eyesight;

as he said of the drawing captioned "Touche" (p. 29) "there is obviously no blood to speak of in the people I draw."

In his stories they bleed and bleed, and without the gloss of the drawings he would be remembered as a sardonic provincial in the Ring Lardner manner—a valuable American tradition in its own right, but Thurber didn't bite clear through like Lardner. Yet the stories plus the drawings give us the extra angle that reveals a genius. The stories are like the engine behind the drawings. Thurber came East with his mouth as wide as Scott Fitzgerald's, and for a while he reveled in what he took to be the glamor of it all. But then under pressure of booze and intelligence the mouth collapsed in a snarl and he became unfathomably bitter. When his eyes closed for good, he lost his most cheerful feature and joined the Lardner-Fitzgerald stream of disappointed Americans—than whom there is no one in the world more disappointed.

But thank God, he compiled this book first, while youthful high spirits could still put funny hats on his nightmares and the intoxication of humorous invention was glamor enough. The dark themes are there in embryo—in especial, the husband and wife who, having exhausted the competition, round on each other for the finals, the death struggle. But he could still be diverted by jokes that had nothing to say about anything, and Thurber is at his best when he isn't saying anything about anything. "I said the hounds of Spring are on Winter's traces, but let it pass, let it pass." I used to repeat this line so often as a boy, that it lost all humor, and finally all meaning, and still I loved it. That's art and that's Thurber.

Later on he became famous, and it's harder to be an artist then. By a cruel coincidence, fame and blindness arrived almost togther so that fame had to do everything for him and he made too much of it. He had once written a story about a kid who flies round the world but is too obnoxious to be a suitable hero, and sadly he proceeded to live out this story himself. Like his aviator, "Pal" Smurch, he didn't know how a great man was supposed to behave, it was so far from natural bent. Worst of all, critics convinced him he had been "saying something" all along, as indeed he had, but now he began saying it consciously, and it was nothing much in that form.

So this book comes just in time to rescue an authentic comic genius from the flat taste of his last works, and from Burton Bernstein's coroner's report of a biography, which no doubt had to be written, but which badly needs a chaser. At a period when jazz had been flattened into swing and the Hays Office sat on Hollywood's head, such as it

13

was, humor was possibly the only American popular art that the rest of the literate world took seriously. And what they saw first and liked best was this strange fuzzy window on the American soul, the drawings of James Thurber.

WILFRID SHEED

PREFACE

I had long ago made my design for what was to become of me when the Reaper had swung his scythe through my neck. I was to be cremated after death—at least, I always trusted it would be after death. I even left instructions to this effect in my will, a document that might otherwise have been writ in a large, schoolgirl backhand on the head of a pin. Now, with the publication of this book, I must change those words, and with them my plans for the long, long rest. Now I want to be left as approximately is, so I may be buried in a prominent place on a travelled thoroughfare through a wildly popular cemetery. Above me I want a big white stone—you will see why it must be big—on which I want carven in clear letters: "Uncover before this dust, for when it was a woman, it was doubly honored. Twice in life, it was given to her below to introduce the work of James Thurber. Reader, who around here, including you, can tie that record?"

I like to think of my shining tombstone. It gives me, as you might say, something to live for.

It gives me, also, a lovely diversion with which to while away eternity. I have always found it best to be quiet and alone with a Thurber drawing, that I may seek to fathom what went on in the lives of the characters depicted, before the artist chose his moment for setting them down forever. Sometimes I wonder if eternity is going to be half long enough for me to make anything near a reasonable guess.

Consider, for instance, the picture showing a man, his wife, and a male guest. They are standing in a something less than gracious enclosure, furnished mainly with a bookcase apparently ordered by mail from the company that did such notable work in Pisa. And on top of the bookcase is a woman on all fours. So help me God, there is a woman on all fours on top of the bookcase. And the host is saying, "That's my first wife up there, and this is the *present* Mrs. Harris."

Well, what would you do about that? I worked for a while on the theory that the first Mrs. Harris, the one on top of the bookcase, was

15

dead and stuffed, but my heart was never really in it. In the first place, she doesn't look stuffed; she looks limp. She looks limp and resigned and only a trifle bewildered. She has the look of having been where she is for a long time. How do they feed her? Do they put a cover over her at night? And what made her husband dispose of her and take his present mate? The new spouse is no more sweetly shaped, no more elegantly clothed, no more carefully coiffed than the old one. They look equally terrible. Could it be that the first wife had a habit of crouching on top of bookcases, and one day he could stand it no longer and said, "Oh, all right, if *that's* what you want to do," and flung out and got married again? What does the new wife, that *present* Mrs. Harris, think of the arrangement? She looks not too sensitive, luckily for her, but she must know, when her friends come in for bridge, that her household is not overly conventional. And the bookcase is full of books. What books, in heaven's name, what books do such people read?

You understand what I mean when I say that eternity will not be long enough for my figuring?

Or take again, for instance, the fine drawing of the court scene—the mild judge, the cocksure lawyer, and the aghast witness. "Perhaps *this* will refresh your memory," the lawyer is saying in his nasty way, as he produces, no doubt with a flourish, a kangaroo—a tender, young, innocent, wistful kangaroo. What, I ask you, what can lie back of that?

I give up such things; or at least I say I do. But I find I keep on working at them through the white nights.

I cannot say that James Thurber's work has progressed. No more could I say that the new moon is more exquisite than the last one. I will not be so illiterate as to expand the perfect into the more perfect.

But I do say I see certain changes in his characters. The men seem to me, in the main, a little smaller, even a little more innocent, even a little more willing to please than before. Also, the *pince nez,* superbly done by a slanted line across the nose, seems to be more widely worn by them. It is to be hoped they do not turn to glasses to obtain a better view of their women. Because the ladies are increasingly awful. They get worse and worse, as we sit here. And there they are behaving, with never a moment's doubt, like *femmes fatales.*

It is hard for me to comment on The War Between Men and Women, for naturally I am partisan because of my sex. It is tough going for me to see the women in retreat, routed; finally to witness the woman general, mounted on that curious horse, doubtless a spy, surrendering her baseball bat to the late enemy. I comforted myself with the fact that no man had equaled the strange wild daring of Mrs. Pritchard's Leap. Then I realized I needed no such comfort. For if you study this glorious battle sequence closely, you will realize that the women, rout or no rout, surrender or no surrender, are the real winners. I suppose I understand that we are licked only when I say I doubt if our victory is for the best.

Mr. Thurber's animals have not changed with his new work; they have just got more so. My heart used to grow soft at the sight of his dogs; now it turns completely liquid. I give you, for the third time in instance, that darling who looks cautiously out his door, curves his paw to the snowstorm, and turns his poor, bewildered head up to the spewing heavens. There is nowhere else existent an innocence like to that of Thurber animals. . . . Even that strange, square beast, beside which lie the neat hat, the cold pipe, the empty shoe, and in front of which stands the stern woman, her hands on her hips, demanding, "What have you done with Dr. Millmoss?". . .

You see how easy it is to say "Thurber animals." The artist has gone into the language. How often we say, "He's a Thurber man" or "Look at that woman—she's a perfect Thurber," and, God help us and them, we are always understood. We need say no more about them. We have been taught to recognize them by the master. Possibly Thurber humans and animals existed before the artist drew them. I am willing to concede that they may have, but I am strong to say that I doubt it. I believe that Nature again has been shown her place, and has gone into her old specialty of imitating art.

Two of my best friends are dogs of a whirling mélange of ancestry. They are short in the paw, long and wavering in the body, heavy and worried in the head. They are willing, useless, and irresistible. Nobody ever asks their breed. "Oh, look at the Thurber dogs," people say who see them for the first time. . . . If I were Mr. Thurber, I should rather have my name used that way even than have it bracketed, as it has so often been, with that of Matisse. . . .

I think you must know how I feel to be in the same book with a fine artist, to be standing here, this moment and forever, presenting his finest work. That is why I choke a little when I say, and with doubled privilege and doubled pride that I may say it again: Ladies and gentlemen, Mr. James Thurber.

DOROTHY PARKER

New York, 1943

17

"Well, *don't* come and look at the rainbow then, you big ape!"

"It's a naïve domestic Burgundy without any breeding, but I think
you'll be amused by its presumption."

"You're going a bit far, Miss Blanchard."

"Bang! Bang! Bang!"

"You gah dam pussy cats!"

"It's Lida Bascom's husband — he's frightfully unhappy."

"What do you want to be inscrutable *for*, Marcia?"

"Look out! Here they come again!"

"I'm afraid you are in the wrong apartment, Madam."

"Why do you keep raising me when you *know* I'm bluffing?"

"Touché!"

"Why don't you wait and see what becomes of your *own* generation
before you jump on mine?"

"There's no use you trying to save *me*, my good man."

"I'm wearing gloves because I don't want to leave any fingerprints around."

"I come from haunts of coot and hern!"

"I was voted the biggest heel in school, Mamma!"

"You and your premonitions!"

"She's reading some novel that's breaking her heart, but we don't
know where she hides it."

"They're going to put you away if you don't quit acting like this."

"You were wonderful at the Gardners' last night, Fred, when you
turned on the charm."

"Oh, Doctor *Conroy* — *look!*"

"You haven't got the face for it, for *one* thing."

"Of course he's terribly nervous, but I'm sure he meant it as a pass at me."

"My husband wanted to live in sin, even *after* we were married."

"Who are you today — Ronald Colman?"

"Here! Here! There's a place for that, sir!"

"Maybe you don't have charm, Lily, but you're enigmatic."

"What have you done with Dr. Millmoss?"

"One of you men in the kitchen give the officer another drink!"

"What do four ones beat?"

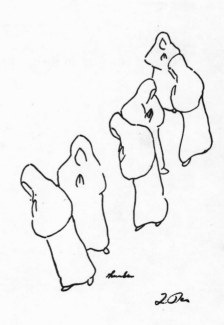

"Good *morning*, my feathered friends!"

"I can't get in touch with your uncle, but there's a horse here that
wants to say hello."

"I'm so glad you're a writer — I'm just full of themes and ideas."

"I drew three more clubs and filled my flush!"

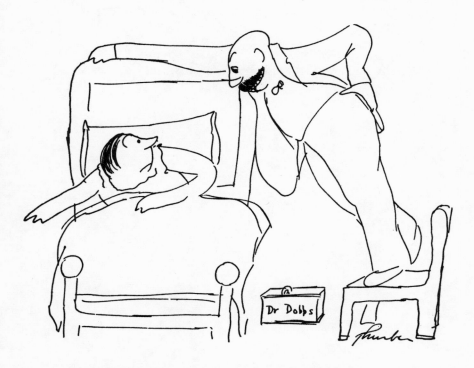

"You're not my patient, you're my meat, Mrs. Quist!"

"Why don't you let *me* know what it is, if it's so pleasant?"

"I'll thank you to keep your mother's name out of this!"

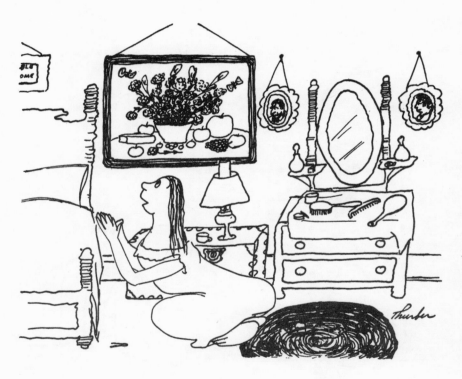

". . . and keep me a normal, healthy girl."

"That martyred look won't get you anywhere with me!"

"This is Miss Jones, Doctor — I want you to cheer her up. She's been through hell recently."

"For Heaven's sake, why don't you go outdoors and trace something?"

59

"I think of you as being enormously alive."

"Ooooo, *guesties!*"

"If you can keep a secret, I'll tell you how my husband died."

"He's been like this ever since Munich."

"What's come over you since Friday, Miss Schemke?"

"Here's to m' first wife, darling — she only wore one hat, God
bless 'er!"

"The trouble with me is I can never say no."

"I'm Virgo with the moon in Aries, if that will help you any."

"There go the most intelligent of all animals."

"My wife had me arrested one night last week."

"Why did I ever marry below my emotional level!"

"One of us ought to be a Boswell, taking this all down."

"I'd feel a great deal easier if her husband hadn't gone to bed."

"And this is Tom Weatherby, an old beau of your mother's. He
never got to first base."

"What the hell ever happened to the old-fashioned love story?"

"Shut up, Prince! What's biting you?"

"I want you to know Mr. Thrawn, Mr. Simms. Mr. Thrawn claims
to be a werewolf."

"My heart has been a stick of wood since May, 1927, Miss Prentice."

"Darling, I seem to have this rabbit."

"He's just heard about the changes that are taking place in civilization."

DESTINATIONS

"I don't know them either, dear, but there may be some very simple explanation."

"I love the idea of there being two sexes, don't you?"

"Yoo-hoo — George! Chanticleer!"

THE ENEMIES

"And *this* is my *father*, Mr. Williams — home from the wars or something."

"I don't want him to be comfortable if he's going to look too funny."

"I can't *stand* to have my pulse felt, Doctor!"

"Well, I'm disenchanted, too. We're *all* disenchanted."

"This is like that awful afternoon we telephoned Mencken."

"You wait here and I'll bring the etchings down."

"Unhappy woman!"

"See you at the barricades, Mr. Whitsonby!"

"Have you seen my pistol, Honey-bun?"

"I wouldn't rent this room to everybody, Mr. Spencer. This is
where my husband lost his mind."

"I don't want any part of it!"

"I'd dread falling under your spell, Mr. Pierson."

"I said the hounds of Spring are on Winter's traces — but let it pass, let it pass!"

"What ever became of the Socialist Party?"

"I wonder what dark flowers grow in the mysterious caverns of your soul."

"I thought you'd enjoy Miss Perrish, darling. She has a constant ringing in *her* ears, too."

"I brought a couple of midgets — do you mind?"

"What do you want me to do with your remains, George?"

"He knows all about art, but he doesn't know what he likes."

"Father would be much happier if you wouldn't."

"This gentleman was kind enough to see me home, darling."

"Well, it makes a difference to *me*!"

"She's all I know about Bryn Mawr and she's all I have to know."

"It's our *own* story *exactly!* He bold as a hawk, she soft as the dawn."

"Miss Gorce is in the embalming game."

"Who is this Hitler and what does he want?"

"I beg to differ with you!"

"Every day is Arbor Day to Mr. Chisholm."

"You said a moment ago that everybody you look at seems to be a
rabbit. Now just what do you mean by that, Mrs. Sprague?"

"I never really rallied after the birth of my first child."

"Other end, Mr. Pemberton."

"Welcome back to the old water hole, Mrs. Bixby!"

"Well, who made the magic go out of our marriage — you or me?"

"Le coeur a ses raisons, Mrs. Bence, que la raison ne connait pas."

"Well, if I called the wrong number, why did you answer
the phone?"

"Would you step over here a second, Waldo? This one's bearing cotton."

"He doesn't believe a single word he's read in the past ten years."

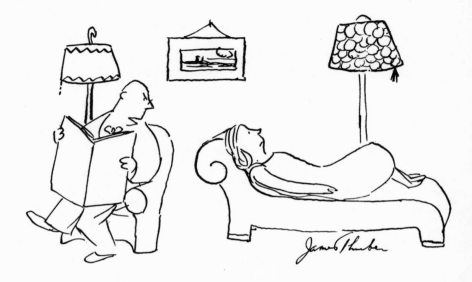

"I do love you. I just don't feel like talking military tactics with you."

"Now I'm going to go in over your horns!"

"Alice can be a little *girl* Commando in your game, Donald."

"Dr. Livingstone, I presume?"

"Yoo-hoo, it's me and the ape man."

"I tell you there isn't going to *be* any insurrection."

"Mother, this is Tristram."

"I'm offering you sanctuary, Dr. Mason."

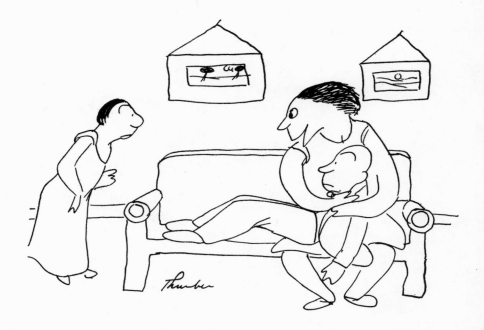

"Your husband has talked about nothing but you, Mrs. Miller."

"With a hey-nonny-nonny and a nuts to you!"

"Which you am I talking to now?"

"You can't *make* me go home!"

"You can tell me if I bend my knees, Sugar."

"The party's breaking up, darling."

"Look out, Harry!"

"Tell her she's *afraid* to come out and fight!"

"This is not the real me you're seeing, Mrs. Clisbie."

"And this is the little woman."

"She's been this way ever since she saw 'Camille.' "

"I assume then, that you regard yourself as omniscient. If I am
wrong, correct me!"

"That's my first wife up there, and this is the *present* Mrs. Harris."

"He's given up everything for a whole year."

"George! If that's you I'll never forgive you!"

"My wife wants to spend Halloween with her first husband."

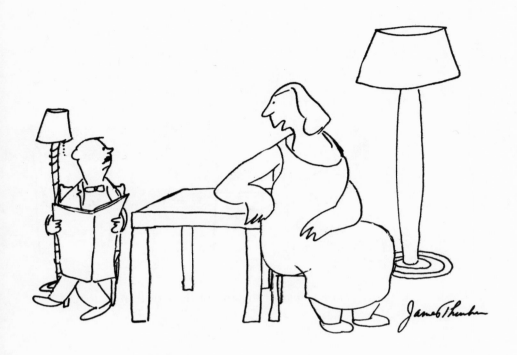

"My analyst is crazy to meet you, darling."

"She predicts either war or the end of the world in October."

"Perhaps *this* will refresh your memory."

"Why, Mr. Spears, how cute you look!"

"Lippmann scares me this morning."

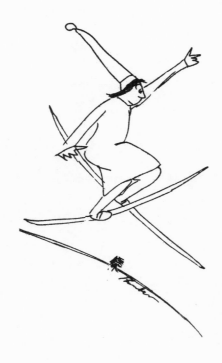

"She says she's burning with a hard, gemlike flame. It's something they learn in school, I think."

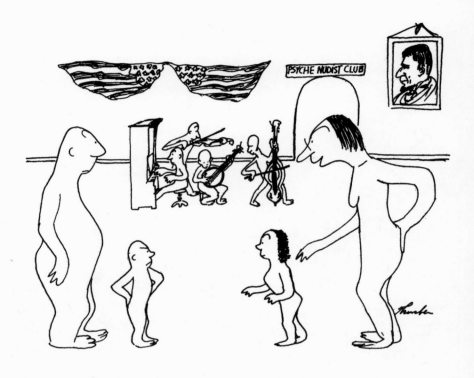

"Dance with the nice man's little boy, dear."

"He's so charming it gives you the creeps."

"Well, you see, the story *really* goes back to when I was a teensy-weensy little girl."

"Do you people mind if I take off some of these hot clothes?"

"Will you please cease calling me Sweetie Pie in public?"

"It goes, 'Build thee some stately mansions, O my soul.' "

"Lots of little men have got somewhere — Napoleon, Dollfuss, Billy Rose."

"She's broken up about this play she saw. Thomas Jefferson loses his wife and four children and Monticello."

"Hello, darling — woolgathering?"

"He doesn't know anything except facts."

"Laissez faire and let laissez faire is what I believe in."

"Why, I never dreamed your union had been blessed with issue!"

"She built up her personality but she's undermined her character."

"He hates people."

"I say she used to be no better than she ought to be, but she is now."

THE LAST FLOWER

"TOBACCO ROAD"

Sundown at the Lesters' house in the grotesquely humorous play at the Forty-eighth Street Theatre, as felt rather than seen by our artist. The characters' souls, or what passes for them, rather than their outward likenesses, are presented here. The bundle of rags on the horizon is Grandma Lester, if not really Patricia Quinn, who plays the part. The other symbols, from right to left, are Margaret Wycherly, Henry Hull, Dean Jagger, Sam Byrd, Reneice Rehan, and Ruth Hunter.

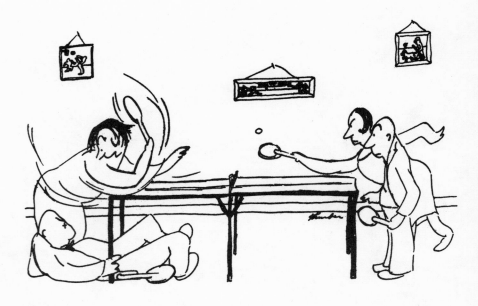

"Sorry, partner!"

"It's Parkins, sir; we're 'aving a bit of a time below stairs."

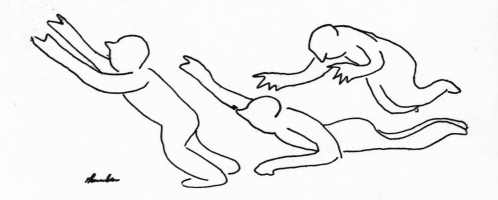

RAIN IN THE DESERT

"I suppose all that you men think about is war."

"So I said to the bank teller, 'How can I be overdrawn when I have all these checks left?' "

"She has the true Emily Dickinson spirit except that she gets fed
up occasionally."

"All right, all right, try it that way! Go ahead and try it that way!"

"They were shot by George's uncle — the one that lost his mind."

"Have you no code, man?"

The Hound and the Hat

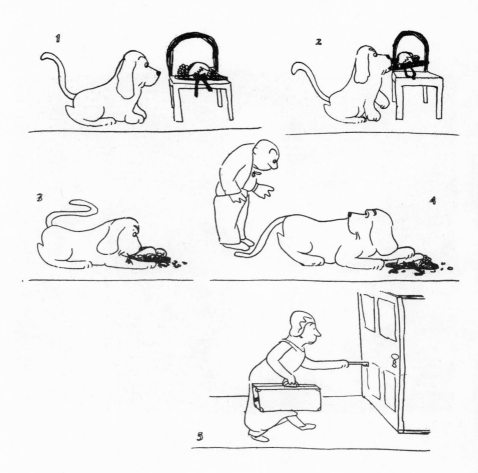

THE MASCULINE APPROACH

The Candy-and-Flowers Campaign

The I'm-Drinking-Myself-to-Death-and-Nobody-Can-Stop-Me
Method

The Strong, Silent System

The Pawing System

The Strange-Fascination Technique

The You'll-Never-See-Me-Again Tactics

The Heroic, or Dangers-I-Have-Known, Method

The Let-'Em-Wait-and-Wonder Plan

The Unhappy-Childhood Story

The Indifference Attitude

The Letter-Writing Method

The Man-of-the-World, or Ordering-in-French, Maneuver

The Sweep-'Em-Off-Their-Feet Method

The Her-Two-Little-Hands-in-His-Huge-Ones Pass

The Sudden Onslaught

The Continental-Manners Technique

The I'm-Not-Good-Enough-for-You Announcement

The Just-a-Little-Boy System

The Harpo Marx Attack

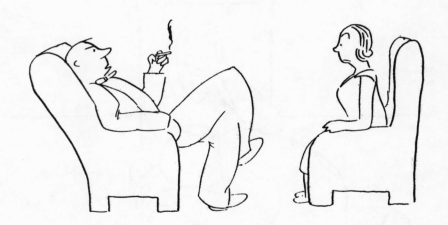

The I-May-Go-Away-for-a-Year-or-Two Move

FIRST AID

"In first-aid class today we learned eleven different ways to poison people."

"Well, you're not going to try the fireman's lift on me!"

"I think he's stopped breathing. What do I do now?"

"How's about going somewhere and trying traction splints on each other, Miss Bryson?"

THE WAR BETWEEN MEN AND WOMEN

I. The Overt Act

II. The Battle on the Stairs

III. The Fight in the Grocery

IV. Men's G.H.Q.

V. Women's G.H.Q.

VI. Capture of three physics professors

VII. Surrender of three blondes

VIII. The Battle of Labrador

IX. The Spy

X. Mrs. Pritchard's Leap

XI. Zero Hour — Connecticut

XII. The Sniper

XIII. Parley

XIV. Gettysburg

XV. Retreat

XVI. Rout

XVII. Surrender